~ BIBLE ~
FLOWERS

~ BIBLE ~
FLOWERS

HARMONY BOOKS
NEW YORK

Introduction copyright © 1996 by Jenny de Gex
Illustrations copyright see page 68

Published by Harmony Books, a division of Crown Publishers, Inc.,
201 East 50th Street, New York, New York 10022.
Member of the Crown Publishing Group.

Random House, Inc. New York, Toronto, London, Sydney, Auckland

HARMONY and colophon are trademarks of Crown Publishers, Inc.
Originally published in Great Britain by Pavilion Books Limited in 1996

Manufactured in Singapore

Text and pictures compiled by Jenny de Gex
Design by David Fordham

Library of Congress Cataloging-in-Publication Data available on request

ISBN 0-517-70412-9

10 9 8 7 6 5 4 3 2 1

First American Edition

Jacket illustrations: British Library, London, *Isabella Breviary*,
Add MS 18851, ff. 146v, 173, 477v

CONTENTS

INTRODUCTION

THE Holy Land in biblical times was, as it is now, mainly desert and arid land, difficult territory for smallholdings or subsistence farming. But the Bible contains many references to plants, fruits, gardens and agriculture, from Genesis to the Gospels.

> 'And God said, "Let the earth put forth vegetation, plants yielding seed and fruit trees bearing fruit in which is their seed, each according to its kind, upon the earth."'
> (GENESIS 1:11).

Many of these references are allegorical or symbolic, but there is no doubt that gardens existed there. They were essentially practical: for fruit, vegetables or herbs, and the trees planted were usually olive, fig or pomegranate. In fact, the name of the garden of Gethsemane, on the Mount of Olives, means 'of the oil press'. The Garden of Eden became known as 'Paradise', an anglicized form of the Persian for a walled garden, depicted in Christian religious art in medieval times as an idealized garden.

Symbolic references to nature in the Bible begin with Adam and Eve in the Garden of Eden, tempted by the serpent to eat forbidden fruit from the tree of knowledge of good and evil. Fruit continues to be an important symbol to theologians, who have suggested that Jesus himself is the fruit of eternal life.

Old Testament texts often mention nature, and frequently refer to flowers, seeds, grass, wheat or herbs. Sometimes references are very specific, for example, hyssop, rue, mint and bay are mentioned by name; plants were always put to practical use, rather than serving any decorative purpose.

Proof of the existence of early gardens is handed down to us in art from the Assyrians, Egyptians, the Greeks and the Romans.

The gardens of the wealthy were provided with water for irrigation; for example, King Solomon's garden had pools:

'I made myself gardens and parks, and planted in them all kinds of fruit trees. I made myself pools from which to water the forests of growing trees.'
(ECCLESIASTES 2:5-6).

References to gardening in the Bible often touch on husbandry:

'I am the true vine . . . Every branch in me that beareth not fruit he taketh away; and every branch that beareth fruit, he purgeth it, that it may bring forth more fruit.'
(JOHN 15:1-2).

'He causeth the grass to grow for the cattle, and herb for the service of man; that he may bring forth food but out of the earth.'
(PSALM 104:14).

Parables that mention vegetation symbolically include those of the sower, of the tares and of mustard seed (all from St Matthew 13):

'But he that received seed into the good ground is he that heareth the word, and understandeth it which also beareth fruit.'

Similar analogies to growth and spiritual harvest have passed into our language and literature:

'A good tree cannot bring forth evil fruit, neither can a corrupt tree bring forth good fruit.'
(ST MATTHEW 7:18).

Translators of biblical texts from the Hebrew had great difficulty deciding on plant identities. The writers were not botanists and their use of plant names was imprecise. For example, the rose mentioned in the Song of Solomon as the rose of Sharon was more likely to be a crocus or narcissus, although wild dog-rose and the

white Phoenician rose grew in the Holy Land. The plant then known as the desert rose is not a rose at all, but a cactus. In the excerpt from Isaiah 35:1 (page 44), the flower might be a rose, a crocus or an asphodel.

Our knowledge of these plants is due to botanists, notably at the Royal Botanic Gardens at Kew in London, who have made detailed field studies of plants proven by archaeological research to have grown in the Holy Land during Christ's lifetime some 2,000 years ago. Some of these still grow there today.

The comparison between a fast-fading flower and the briefness of human life features several times in the Bible:

> *'All flesh is grass, and all its beauty is like the flower of the field.'*
> (ISAIAH 40:6)

These 'flowers of the field' may have meant any wild flowers, so no specific identifications can be made. However, amongst those widespread in the Mediterranean region are anemone, poppy, crown daisy and camomile, which, coincidentally, also featured as decoration on the borders of medieval illuminated manuscripts.

In the Song of Solomon 2:12, reference is made, according to botanists, to the mountain tulip, *Tulipa montana*:

'The flowers appear on the earth, the time of singing has come,
and the voice of the turtledove is heard in our land.'

As well as the mountain tulip, and the roses mentioned earlier, Star of Bethlehem, rock roses, myrtle, mint (mentioned by Jesus in Matthew 23:23) and rue also grew in the Holy Land, as did hyssop (*Origanum syriacum*), a herb mentioned by name in the Bible. It was used for sprinkling blood on the door lintels and posts at the time of the Passover, and was also burnt during sacrifices in the Tabernacle.

As well as herbs, spices such as coriander, saffron and cinnamon occur in the Bible, and the natural riches of the area are reflected in the treasures brought by the three wise men to the infant Jesus: gold, frankincense and myrrh (Matthew 2:11).

Lilies, mentioned in the Song of Solomon, would have been rare in Carmel and Galilee but were common in Minoan art in Crete and are depicted at Knossos. The lily symbolized purity from the earliest days, and may have been grown by the Hebrews for the same reason. In medieval times, the white madonna lily (*Lilium candidum*) became the icon most usually adopted by artists to depict the perfect purity of the Virgin Mary. It became known as a sacred flower, and is used in Christian church flower arrangements to this day. Like the lily, many flowers came to have iconographic significance, and were associated with individual saints, who were then recognizable in all forms of art by their emblems.

This small volume will not enter into the complex theological debates concerning the seed and the Word (of God). Instead, selected passages from the Bible either refer to flowers or have been chosen to match a particularly fine example of medieval manuscript illumination, even if the text has no floral connection. This book is therefore intended to serve as a decorative source of pleasure or contemplation. It follows the medieval tradition of Books of Hours, for which patrons commissioned illuminations.

The Book of Hours was a prayer book for the lay reader, and its popularity grew with the growth of literacy. Miniature in size, it contained prayers and Offices or Hours, Penitential Psalms, the Litany, the Office of the Dead, the Gradual Psalms, and extracts from the Bible. Breviaries were similarly illustrated, and contained texts for the recitation of the eight services which make up the daily office of the Catholic Church. The most richly decorated manuscripts were created in the fourteenth to sixteenth centuries by Flemish, French and Italian masters and their studios, initially under noble patronage but later reaching wider audiences.

The illustrations in this book have been chosen mainly from two manuscripts of major importance. The *Isabella Breviary* was written and illuminated in Flanders, probably in Bruges, during the last decade of the fifteenth century, for Queen Isabella of Castile. One of the most influential figures in Europe, she was also patron of Columbus' voyage to America in 1492. It was presented to her around 1497 to commemorate the marriages of two of her children to the son and daughter of Maximilian of Austria and his first wife, Duchesss Mary of Burgundy. The manuscript was removed from the Escorial Palace in Madrid during the French invasion of Spain and via private ownership came, in the late nineteenth century, to the British Museum, now the British Library in London.

The second manuscript is the *Hours of Engelbert of Nassau*, produced by an artist known as the Master of Mary of Burgundy, who painted masterpieces for the Duchess. The *Hours* belonged to Mary's son, Philip the Fair, who passed the book to Engelbert as a gift, in recognition of his attempts to resist the French seizure of parts of the Netherlands in the turmoil following Mary's death.

The particular skill of this artist was to use *trompe l'oeil*, making the manuscript appear as if it has flowers scattered on the page. He combined borders with miniatures and script into a unified whole. The flowers are in minute detail, almost as if magnified and three-dimensional.

The essence of *Bible Flowers* is distilled in the illustrated morning prayer by the Master of the Prayer Book (page 17), dating from around 1500. It represents a medieval Christian ideal, that of dedicating the day to God immediately upon waking. Those that believed, believed fervently.

Political and religious turmoil over the last few thousand years has given the Holy Land a troubled and often violent history. In this book the enduring words of the Bible, despite its many translations, are combined with the visions of medieval artists inspired by belief in a universal truth, to make a modern-day Book of Hours.

Symbolism and poetry compare the natural world around us, shown in rich illuminations, reminding us we are mere mortals:

> *'For all flesh is as grass, and all the glory of man as the flower of grass. The grass withereth and the flower thereof falleth away. But the word of the Lord endureth for ever.'*
> (I PETER 1:24-5)

JENNY DE GEX

1995

Quando surgere delecto, dic oratio
sequentem. Oratio
urrexit dominus de
sepulchro. qui pro no
bis pependit i ligno

GENESIS

AND God said, Let there be a firmament in the midst of the waters, and let it divide the waters from the waters.

7 And God made the firmament, and divided the waters which *were* under the firmament from the waters which *were* above the firmament: and it was so.

8 And God called the firmament Heaven. And the evening and the morning were the second day.

9 And God said, Let the waters under the heaven be gathered together unto one place, and let the dry *land* appear: and it was so.

10 And God called the dry *land* Earth; and the gathering together of the waters called he Seas: and God saw that *it was* good.

11 And God said, Let the earth bring forth grass, the herb yielding seed, *and* the fruit tree yielding fruit after his kind, whose seed *is* in itself, upon the earth: and it was so.

12 And the earth brought forth grass, *and* herb yielding seed after his kind, and the tree yielding fruit, whose seed *was* in itself, after his kind: and God saw that *it was* good.

13 And the evening and the morning were the third day.

GENESIS

So God created man in his *own* image, in the image of God created he him; male and female created he them.

28 And God blessed them, and God said unto them, Be fruitful, and multiply, and replenish the earth, and subdue it: and have dominion over the fish of the sea, and over the fowl of the air, and over every living thing that moveth upon the earth.

29 And God said, Behold, I have given you every herb bearing seed, which *is* upon the face of all the earth, and every tree, in the which *is* the fruit of a tree yielding seed; to you it shall be for meat.

30 And to every beast of the earth, and to every fowl of the air, and to every thing that creepeth upon the earth, wherein *there is* life, *I have given* every green herb for meat: and it was so.

31 And God saw every thing that he had made, and, behold, *it was* very good. And the evening and the morning were the sixth day.

onuerte nos deus
salutaris nr.
Et auerte iram
tuam a nobis.
eus in adiuto
rium meum intende.
omine ad adiuuandum me fe
stina.
loria patri et filio et spiritu
santto.
icut erat in principio et nuc
et semper et. Psalmus.
epe expugnauerunt me a
inuentute mea: dicat nuc
israel
epe expugnauerunt me a iu
uentute mea. et enim non potuerut
mchi.
upra dorsum meum fabrica
uerunt peccatores: prolonguauerunt
inquitatem suam.
ominus iustus concidet ceru

GENESIS

Thus the heavens and earth were finished, and all the host of them.

2 And on the seventh day God ended his work which he had made; and he rested on the seventh day from all his work which he had made.

3 And God blessed the seventh day, and sanctified it; because that in it he had rested from all his work which God created and made.

4 These *are* the generations of the heavens and of the earth when they were created, in the day that the Lord God made the earth and the heavens,

5 And every plant of the field before it was in the earth, and every herb of the field before it grew: for the Lord God had not caused it to rain upon the earth, and *there was* not a man to till the ground.

6 But there went up a mist from the earth, and watered the whole face of the ground.

7 And the Lord God formed man *of* the dust of the ground, and breathed into his nostrils the breath of life; and man became a living soul.

8 And the Lord God planned a garden eastward in Eden; and there he put the man whom he had formed.

9 And out of the ground made the Lord God to grow every tree that is pleasant to the sight, and good for food; the tree of life also in the midst of the garden, and the tree of knowledge of good and evil.

Deuteronomy

Aʟʟ the commandments which I command thee this day shall ye observe to do, that ye may live, and multiply, and go in and possess the land which the Lord sware unto your fathers.

2 And thou shalt remember all the way which the Lord thy God led thee these forty years in the wilderness, to humble thee, *and* to prove thee, to know what *was* in thine heart, whether thou wouldest keep his commandments, or no.

3 And he humbled thee, and suffered thee to hunger, and fed thee with manna, which thou knewest not, neither did thy fathers know; that he might make thee know that man doth not live by bread only, but by every *word* that proceedeth out of the mouth of the Lord doth man live.

4 Thy raiment waxed not old upon thee, neither did thy foot swell, these forty years.

5 Thou shalt also consider in thine heart, that, as a man chasteneth his son, *so* the Lord thy God chasteneth thee.

6 Therefore thou shalt keep the commandments of the Lord thy God, to walk in his ways, and to fear him.

7 For the Lord thy God bringeth thee into a good land, a land of brooks of water, of fountains and depths that spring out of valleys and hills;

8 A land of wheat, and barley, and vines, and fig trees, and pomegranates; a land of oil olive, and honey;

9 A land wherein thou shalt eat bread without scarceness, thou shalt not lack any *thing* in it; a land whose stones *are* iron, and out of whose hills thou mayest dig brass.

10 When thou hast eaten and art full, then thou shalt bless the Lord thy God for the good land which he hath given thee.

Ad matutinas
de sancto
spiri-
tu.

J OB

F OR we *are but of* yesterday, and know nothing, because our days upon earth *are* a shadow:)

10 Shall not they teach thee, *and* tell thee, and utter words out of their heart?

11 Can the rush grow up without mire? can the flag grow without water?

12 Whilst it *is* yet in his greenness, *and* not cut down, it withereth before any *other* herb.

13 So *are* the paths of all that forget God; and the hypocrite's hope shall perish:

14 Whose hope shall be cut off, and whose trust *shall be* a spider's web.

15 He shall lean upon his house, but it shall not stand: he shall hold it fast, but it shall not endure.

16 He *is* green before the sun, and his branch shooteth forth in his garden.

17 His roots are wrapped about the heap, *and* seeth the place of stones.

18 If he destroy him from his place, then *it* shall deny him, *saying*, I have not seen thee.

19 Behold, this *is* the joy of his way, and out of the earth shall others grow.

20 Behold, God will not cast away a perfect *man*, neither will he help the evil doers:

21 Till he fill thy mouth with laughing, and thy lips with rejoicing.

22 They that hate thee shall be clothed with shame; and the dwelling place of the wicked shall come to nought.

PSALMS

THE earth *is* the Lord's, and the fulness thereof; the world, and they that dwell therein.

2 For he hath founded it upon the seas, and established it upon the floods.

3 Who shall ascend into the hill of the Lord? or who shall stand in his holy place?

4 He that hath clean hands, and a pure heart; who hath not lifted up his soul unto vanity, nor sworn deceitfully.

5 He shall receive the blessing from the Lord, and righteousness from the God of his salvation.

6 This *is* the generation of them that seek him, that seek thy face, O Jacob. Selah.

7 Lift up your heads, O ye gates; and be ye lift up, ye everlasting doors; and the King of glory shall come in.

8 Who *is* this King of glory? The Lord strong and mighty, the Lord mighty in battle.

9 Lift up your heads, O ye gates; even lift *them* up, ye everlasting doors; and the King of glory shall come in.

10 Who is this King of glory? The Lord of hosts, he *is* the King of glory. Selah.

PSALMS

FRET not thyself because of evil-doers, neither be thou envious against the workers of iniquity.

2 For they shall soon be cut down like the grass, and wither as the green herb.

3 Trust in the Lord, and do good; *so* shalt thou dwell in the land, and verily thou shalt be fed.

4 Delight thyself also in the Lord; and he shall give thee the desires of thine heart.

5 Commit thy way unto the Lord; trust also in him; and he shall bring *it* to pass.

6 And he shall bring forth thy righteousness as the light, and thy judgment as the noonday.

7 Rest in the Lord, and wait patiently for him: fret not thyself because of him who prospereth in his way, because of the man who bringeth wicked devices to pass.

8 Cease from anger, and forsake wrath: fret not thyself in any wise to do evil.

9 For evildoers shall be cut off: but those that wait upon the Lord, they shall inherit the earth.

10 For yet a little while, and the wicked *shall* not *be*: yea, thou shalt diligently consider his place, and it *shall* not *be*.

11 But the meek shall inherit the earth; and shall delight themselves in the abundance of peace.

12 The wicked plotteth against the just, and gnasheth upon him with his teeth.

13 The Lord shall laugh at him: for he seeth that his day is coming.

feria quita Innitato Adorem
dominum quinze fecit nos Ant
 venite
Aluum
me facie
tuus
qui in
trauei ei
aque
vsq3 ad animam meam

nfirus sum i tumop
timeli · e non est substanā
Sein at atudinem
mans · e tempestas dume
sit me
Laboraui clamas rau
ce facte sunt fauces meas de
fecerunt oculi mei du speto
in deum meum
Vltiplicati sunt su

PSALMS

*I*T *is a* good *thing* to give thanks unto the Lord, and to sing praises unto thy name, O most High:

2 To shew forth thy lovingkindness in the morning, and thy faithfulness every night,

3 Upon an instrument of ten strings, and upon the psaltery; upon the harp with a solemn sound.

4 For thou, Lord, hast made me glad through thy work: I will triumph in the works of thy hands.

5 O Lord, how great are thy works! *and* thy thoughts are very deep.

6 A brutish man knoweth not; neither doth a fool understand this.

7 When the wicked spring as the grass, and when all the workers of iniquity do flourish; *it is* that they shall be destroyed for ever:

8 But thou, Lord, *art most* high for evermore.

9 For, lo, thine enemies, O Lord, for, lo, thine enemies shall perish; all the workers of iniquity shall be scattered.

10 But my horn shalt thou exalt like *the horn of* an unicorn: I shall be anointed with fresh oil.

11 Mine eye also shall see *my desire* on mine enemies, *and* mine ears shall hear *my desire* of the wicked that rise up against me.

12 The righteous shall flourish like the palm tree: he shall grow like a cedar in Lebanon.

13 Those that be planted in the house of the Lord shall flourish in the courts of our God.

14 They shall still bring forth fruit in old age; they shall be fat and flourishing;

15 To shew that the Lord *is* upright: *he is* my rock, and *there is* no unrighteousness in him.

PSALMS

O SING unto the Lord a new song; for he hath done marvellous things: his right hand, and his holy arm, hath gotten him the victory.

2 The Lord hath made known his salvation: his righteousness hath he openly shewed in the sight of the heathen.

3 He hath remembered his mercy and his truth toward the house of Israel: all the ends of the earth have seen the salvation of our God.

4 Make a joyful noise unto the Lord, all the earth: make a loud noise, and rejoice, and sing praise.

5 Sing unto the Lord, with the harp; with the harp, and the voice of a psalm.

6 With trumpets and sound of cornet make a joyful noise before the Lord, the King.

7 Let the sea roar, and the fulness thereof; the world, and they that dwell therein.

8 Let the floods clap *their* hands: let the hills be joyful together

9 Before the Lord; for he cometh to judge the earth: with righteousness shall he judge the world, and the people with equity.

PSALMS

BLESS the Lord, O my soul and all that is within me, *bless* his holy name.

2 Bless the Lord, O my soul, and forget not all his benefits:

3 Who forgiveth all thine iniquities; who healeth all thy diseases;

4 Who redeemeth thy life from destruction; who crowneth thee with lovingkindness and tender mercies;

5 Who satisfieth thy mouth with good *things; so that* thy youth is renewed like the eagle's.

6 The Lord executeth righteousness and judgment for all that are oppressed.

7 He made known his ways unto Moses, his acts unto the children of Israel.

8 The Lord *is* merciful and gracious, slow to anger, and plenteous in mercy.

9 He will not always chide: neither will he keep *his anger* for ever.

10 He hath not dealt with us after our sins; nor rewarded us according to our iniquities.

11 For as the heaven is high above the earth, *so* great is his mercy toward them that fear him.

12 As far as the east is from the west, *so* far hath he removed our transgressions from us.

13 Like as a father pitieth *his* children, *so* the Lord pitieth them that fear him.

14 For he knoweth our frame; he remembereth that we *are* dust.

15 *As for* man, his days *are* as grass: as a flower of the field, so he flourisheth.

16 For the wind passeth over it, and it is gone; and the place thereof shall know it no more.

Incipiunt septem psalmi penitentiales. Ant. Ne reminiscaris domine.

Domine. Psalmus. Domine ne in furore tuo arguas me neque in ira tua corripias me. Miserere mei domine quoniam infirmus sum sana me domine. quoniam conturbata sunt omnia ossa mea. Et anima mea turbata est valde. sz tu domine usque quo. Convertere domine et eripe animam meam. saluum me fac propter misericordiam tuam. Quoniam non est in morte qui memor sit tui in inferno aut quis confitebitur tibi. Laboraui in gemitu meo lauabo per singulas noctes lectum meum lacrimis

PSALMS

THY testimonies *are* wonderful: therefore doth my soul keep them.

130 The entrance of thy words giveth light; it giveth understanding unto the simple.

131 I opened my mouth, and panted: for I longed for thy commandments.

132 Look thou upon me, and be merciful unto me, as thou usest to do unto those that love thy name.

133 Order my steps in thy word: and let not any iniquity have dominion over me.

134 Deliver me from the oppression of man: so will I keep thy precepts.

135 Make thy face to shine upon thy servant; and teach me thy statutes.

136 Rivers of waters run down mine eyes, because they keep not thy law.

137 Righteous *art* thou, O Lord, and upright *are* thy judgments.

138 Thy testimonies *that* thou hast commanded *are* righteous and very faithful.

139 My zeal hath consumed me, because mine enemies have forgotten thy words.

140 Thy word *is* very pure: therefore thy servant loveth it.

141 I *am* small and despised: *yet* do not I forget thy precepts.

142 Thy righteousness *is* an everlasting righteousness, and thy law *is* the truth.

143 Trouble and anguish have taken hold on me: *yet* thy commandments *are* my delights.

144 The righteousness of thy testimonies *is* everlasting: give me understanding, and I shall live.

39

ECCLESIASTES

CHAPTER I

V.1-11

THE words of the Preacher, the son of David, king in Jerusalem.

2 Vanity of vanities, saith the Preacher, vanity of vanities; all *is* vanity.

3 What profit hath a man of all his labour which he taketh under the sun?

4 *One* generation passeth away, and *another* generation cometh: but the earth abideth for ever.

5 The sun also ariseth, and the sun goeth down, and hasteth to his place where he arose.

6 The wind goeth toward the south, and turneth about unto the north; it whirleth about continually, and the wind returneth again according to his circuits.

7 All the rivers run into the sea; yet the sea *is* not full; unto the place from whence the rivers come, thither they return again.

8 All things *are* full of labour; man cannot utter *it*: the eye is not satisfied with seeing, nor the ear filled with hearing.

9 The thing that hath been, it *is that* which shall be; and that which is done *is* that which shall be done: and *there is* no new *thing* under the sun.

10 Is there *any* thing whereof it may be said, See, this *is* new? it hath been already of old time, which was before us.

11 *There is* no remembrance of former *things*; neither shall there be *any* remembrance of *things* that are to come with *those* that shall come after.

THE SONG OF SOLOMON

I AM the rose of Sharon, *and* the *lily* of the valleys.

2 As the lily among thorns, so *is* my love among the daughters.

3 As the apple tree among the trees of the wood, so *is* my beloved among the sons. I sat down under his shadow with great delight, and his fruit *was* sweet to my taste.

4 He brought me to the banqueting house, and his banner over me *was* love.

5 Stay me with flagons, comfort me with apples: for I *am* sick of love.

6 His left hand *is* under my head, and his right hand doth embrace me.

7 I charge you, O ye daughters of Jerusalem, by the roes, and by the hinds of the field, that ye stir not up, nor awake *my* love, till he please.

8 The voice of my beloved! behold, he cometh leaping upon the mountains, skipping upon the hills.

9 My beloved is like a roe or a young hart: behold, he standeth behind our wall, he looketh forth at the windows, shewing himself through the lattice.

10 My beloved spake, and said unto me, Rise up, my love, my fair one, and come away.

11 For, lo, the winter is past, the rain is over *and* gone;

12 The flowers appear on the earth; the time of the singing *of birds* is come, and the voice of the turtle is heard in our land.

Ilexi quoniam exau
dict dominus voc
oronis mee.
Quia inclinauit
aurem suam michi:
et in diebus meis inuocabo.
Circundederunt me dolores mortis
et pericula inferni inuenerunt me.
Tribulationem et dolorem inue
ni: et nomen domini inuocaui.
O domine libera animam meam
misericors dominus et iustus et deus
nr misertur.
Custodiens paruulos dominus
humiliatus sum et liberauit me.
Conuertere anima mea in requie
tuam: quia dominus benefecit tibi.
Quia eripuit animam meam de
morte oculos meos a lachrimis: pedes
meos a lapsu.
Placebo domino: in regione uiuor.
requiem eternam dona eis dne:

ISAIAH

THE wilderness and the solitary place shall be glad for them; and the desert shall rejoice, and blossom as the rose.

2 It shall blossom abundantly, and rejoice even with joy and singing: the glory of Lebanon shall be given unto it, the excellency of Carmel and Sharon, they shall see the glory of the Lord, *and* the excellency of our God.

3 Strengthen ye the weak hands, and confirm the feeble knees.

4 Say to them *that are* of a fearful heart, Be strong, fear not: behold, your God will come *with* vengeance, *even* God *with* a recompence; he will come and save you.

5 Then the eyes of the blind shall be opened, and the ears of the deaf shall be unstopped.

6 Then shall the lame *man* leap as an hart, and the tongue of the dumb sing: for in the wilderness shall waters break out, and streams in the desert.

7 And the parched ground shall become a pool, and the thirsty land springs of water: in the habitation of dragons, where each lay, *shall be* grass with reeds and rushes.

8 And an highway shall be there, and a way, and it shall be called The way of holiness; the unclean shall not pass over it; but it *shall be* for those: the wayfaring men, though fools, shall not err *therein*.

9 No lion shall be there, nor *any* ravenous beast shall go up thereon, it shall not be found there; but the redeemed shall walk *there*:

10 And the ransomed of the Lord shall return, and come to Zion with songs and everlasting joy upon their heads: they shall obtain joy and gladness, and sorrow and sighing shall flee away.

ISAIAH

COMFORT ye, comfort ye my people, saith your God.

2 Speak ye comfortably to Jerusalem, and cry unto her, that her warfare is accomplished, that her iniquity is pardoned: for she hath received of the Lord's hand double for all her sins.

3 The voice of him that crieth in the wilderness, Prepare ye the way of the Lord, make straight in the desert a highway for our God.

4 Every valley shall be exalted, and every mountain and hill shall be made low: and the crooked shall be made straight, and the rough places plain:

5 And the glory of the Lord shall be revealed, and all flesh shall see *it* together: for the mouth of the Lord hath spoken *it*.

6 The voice said, Cry. And he said, What shall I cry? All flesh *is* grass, and all the goodliness thereof *is* as the flower of the field:

7 The grass withereth, the flower fadeth: because the spirit of the Lord bloweth upon it: surely the people *is* grass.

8 The grass withereth, the flower fadeth: but the word of our God shall stand for ever.

ostend te
domina
mea faū
matrat
mater dō
mini nostri ihu xpi
pietate plenissima
summi regis filia.
mater gloriosissima
mater orphanorum
consolatio desolato
rum via errantium
Salus in te sperau
tium. mundo ante p

47

St Luke

And in the sixth month the angel Gabriel was sent from God unto a city of Galilee, named Nazareth,

27 To a virgin espoused to a man whose name was Joseph, of the house of David; and the virgin's name *was* Mary.

28 And the angel came in unto her, and said, Hail, *thou that art* highly favoured, the Lord *is* with thee: blessed *art* thou among women.

29 And when she saw *him*, she was troubled at his saying, and cast in her mind what manner of salutation this should be.

30 And the angel said unto her, Fear not, Mary: for thou hast found favour with God.

31 And, behold, thou shalt conceive in thy womb, and bring forth a son, and shalt call his name Jesus.

32 He shall be great, and shall be called the Son of the Highest: and the Lord God shall give unto him the throne of his father David:

33 And he shall reign over the house of Jacob for ever; and of his kingdom there shall be no end.

34 Then said Mary unto the angel, How shall this be, seeing I know not a man?

35 And the angel answered and said unto her, The Holy Ghost shall come upon thee, and the power of the Highest shall overshadow thee; therefore also that holy thing which shall be born of thee shall be called the Son of God.

36 And, behold, thy cousin Elisabeth, she hath also conceived a son in her old age: and this is the sixth month with her, who was called barren.

37 For with God nothing shall be impossible.

38 And Mary said, Behold the handmaid of the Lord; be it unto me according to thy word. And the angel departed from her.

St Matthew

Now the birth of Jesus Christ was on this wise: When as his mother Mary was espoused to Joseph, before they came together, she was found with child of the Holy Ghost.

19 Then Joseph her husband, being a just *man*, and not willing to make her a publick example, was minded to put her away privily.

20 But while he thought on these things, behold, the angel of the Lord appeared unto him in a dream, saying, Joseph, thou son of David, fear not to take unto thee Mary thy wife: for that which is conceived in her is of the Holy Ghost.

21 And she shall bring forth a son, and thou shalt call his name Jesus: for he shall save his people from their sins.

22 Now all this was done, that it might be fulfilled which was spoken of the Lord by the prophet, saying,

23 Behold, a virgin shall be with child, and shall bring forth a son, and they shall call his name Emmanuel, which being interpreted is, God with us.

24 Then Joseph being raised from sleep did as the angel of the Lord had bidden him, and took unto him his wife:

25 And knew her not till she had brought forth her firstborn son: and he called his name Jesus.

St Matthew

Now when Jesus was born in Bethlehem of Judæa in the days of Herod the king, behold, there came wise men from the east to Jerusalem.

2 Saying, Where is he that is born King of the Jews? for we have seen his star in the east, and are come to worship him.

3 When Herod the king had heard *these things*, he was troubled, and all Jerusalem with him.

4 And when he had gathered all the chief priests and scribes of the people together, he demanded of them where Christ should be born.

5 And they said unto him, In Bethlehem of Judæa: for thus it is written by the prophet,

6 And thou Bethlehem, *in* the land of Juda, art not the least among the princes of Juda: for out of thee shall come a Governor, that shall rule my people Israel.

7 Then Herod, when he had privily called the wise men, enquired of them diligently what time the star appeared.

8 And he sent them to Bethlehem, and said, Go and search diligently for the young child; and when ye have found *him*, bring me word again, that I may come and worship him also.

9 When they had heard the king, they departed; and, lo, the star, which they saw in the east, went before them, till it came and stood over where the young child was.

10 When they saw the star, they rejoiced with exceeding great joy.

11 And when they were come into the house, they saw the young child with Mary his mother, and fell down, and worshipped him: and when they had opened their treasures, they presented unto him gifts; gold, and frankincense, and myrrh.

FRA
TRES
Multi
pharie,
multisq̃
modis o
lim DE
V S lo
quens pa
tribus in prophetis: nouissime
diebus istis loquutus est nobis
in filio, quem constituit here
dem vniuersorum, per quem
fecit et secula. Qui qum sit
splendor glorie. et figura sub
stantie. eius. portansq̃ omnia

DOMINVS MIHI
ADVITOR

ALLEL ADVITOR
DOMINV

St Luke

And there were in the same country shepherds abiding in the field, keeping watch over their flock by night.

9 And, lo, the angel of the Lord came upon them, and the glory of the Lord shone round about them: and they were sore afraid.

10 And the angel said unto them, Fear not: for, behold, I bring you good tidings of great joy, which shall be to all people.

11 For unto you is born this day in the city of David a Saviour, which is Christ the Lord.

12 And this *shall be* a sign unto you; Ye shall find the babe wrapped in swaddling clothes, lying in a manger.

13 And suddenly there was with the angel a multitude of the heavenly host praising God, and saying,

14 Glory to God in the highest and on earth peace, good will toward men.

15 And it came to pass, as the angels were gone away from them into heaven, the shepherds said one to another, Let us now go even unto Bethlehem, and see this thing which is come to pass, which the Lord hath made known unto us.

16 And they came with haste, and found Mary, and Joseph, and the babe lying in a manger.

17 And when they had seen *it*, they made known abroad the saying which was told them concerning this child.

18 And all they that heard *it* wondered at those things which were told them by the shepherds.

19 But Mary kept all these things, and pondered *them* in her heart.

20 And the shepherds returned, glorifying and praising God for all the things that they had heard and seen, as it was told unto them.

ST MATTHEW

No man can serve two masters: for either he will hate the one, and love the other; or else he will hold to the one, and despise the other. Ye cannot serve God and mammon.

25 Therefore I say unto you, Take no thought for your life, what ye shall eat, or what ye shall drink; nor yet for your body, what ye shall put on. Is not the life more than meat, and the body than raiment?

26 Behold the fowls of the air: for they sow not, neither do they reap, nor gather into barns; yet your heavenly Father feedeth them. Are ye not much better than they?

27 Which of you by taking thought can add one cubit unto his stature?

28 And why take ye thought for raiment? Consider the lilies of the field, how they grow; they toil not neither do they spin:

29 And yet I say unto you, That even Solomon in all his glory was not arrayed like one of these.

30 Wherefore, if God so clothe the grass of the field, which to day is, and to morrow is cast into the oven, *shall he* not much more *clothe* you, O ye of little faith?

31 Therefore take no thought, saying, What shall we eat? or, What shall we drink? or, Wherewithal shall we be clothed?

32 (For after all these things did the Gentiles seek:) for your heavenly Father knoweth that ye have need of all these things.

33 But seek ye first the kingdom of God, and his righteousness; and all these things shall be added unto you.

34 Take therefore no thought for the morrow: for the morrow shall take thought for the things of itself. Sufficient unto the day *is* the evil thereof.

Ad vinam

Deus in ad
iutorium
meum in
tende. Do
mine ad

adiuuandum me festina.

Gloria patri et filio et
spiritui sancto. Sicut erat
in principio et nunc et semp
et in secula seculorum amen

Uem arator spū vim
mentes tuorum vi
sita implse superna gracia
que tu arasti pectora

Memento salutis auc

ST LUKE

AND Jesus being full of the Holy Ghost returned from Jordan, and was led by the Spirit into the wilderness,

2 Being forty days tempted of the devil. And in those days he did eat nothing: and when they were ended, he afterward hungered.

3 And the devil said unto him, If thou be the Son of God, command this stone that it be made bread.

4 And Jesus answered him, saying, It is written, That man shall not live by bread alone, but by every word of God.

5 And the devil, taking him up into an high mountain, shewed unto him all the kingdoms of the world in a moment of time.

6 And the devil said unto him, All this power will I give thee, and the glory of them: for that is delivered unto me; and to whomsoever I will I give it.

7 If thou therefore wilt worship me, all shall be thine.

8 And Jesus answered and said unto him, Get thee behind me, Satan: for it is written, Thou shalt worship the Lord thy God, and him only shalt thou serve.

9 And he brought him to Jerusalem, and set him on a pinnacle of the temple, and said unto him, If thou be the Son of God, cast thyself down from hence:

10 For it is written, He shall give his angels charge over thee, to keep thee:

11 And in *their* hands they shall bear thee up, lest at any time thou dash thy foot against a stone.

12 And Jesus answering said unto him, It is said, Thou shalt not tempt the Lord thy God.

13 And when the devil had ended all the temptation, he departed from him for a season.

ST MATTHEW

AND as they were eating, Jesus took bread, and blessed *it*, and brake *it*, and gave *it* to the disciples, and said, Take, eat; this is my body.

27 And he took the cup, and gave thanks, and gave *it* to them, saying, Drink ye all of it;

28 For this is my blood of the new testament, which is shed for many for the remission of sins.

29 But I say unto you, I will not drink henceforth of this fruit of the vine, until that day when I drink it new with you in my Father's kingdom.

30 And when they had sung an hymn, they went out into the mount of Olives.

31 Then saith Jesus unto them, All ye shall be offended because of me this night: for it is written, I will smite the shepherd, and the sheep of the flock shall be scattered abroad.

32 But after I am risen again, I will go before you into Galilee.

33 Peter answered and said unto him, Though all *men* shall be offended because of thee, *yet* will I never be offended.

34 Jesus said unto him, Verily I say unto thee, That this night, before the cock crow, thou shalt deny me thrice.

35 Peter said unto him, Though I should die with thee, yet will I not deny thee. Likewise also said all the disciples.

36 Then cometh Jesus with them unto a place called Gethsemane, and saith unto the disciples, Sit ye here, while I go and pray yonder.

hanc familiam tuã pro qua
dñs nr̃ ihs xp̃s non dubita
uit manib; tradi nocentiũ
z crucis subire tormentum
Amẽ. Cõpleti solito more
absq; prostratione dicatur
benedictio propter dcm̃ In
duob; uero sequentib; nõ vel
benedictio Ant̃ ve beata mri
ne. hac die z duob; seq̃ntib;

non dicatur. Ad matutina
Inuitatorui̇ nõ dicatur. Do
mine labia nec ver̃ in aduẽt
neq; inuitatoriũ in ynõ. s; ver̃
Pater nr̃ z Credo. postq̃; sig
hauerint se fratres. q̃i eciã
hat ad alias horas. statim
incipiatur. In primo noct̃
no. Antiphona. z hic in
cipitur: ꝗꝗꝗꝗ ꝗꝗꝗ

St Matthew

And while he yet spake, lo, Judas, one of the twelve, came, and with him a great multitude with swords and staves, from the chief priests and elders of the people.

48 Now he that betrayed him gave them a sign, saying, Whomsoever I shall kiss, that same is he: hold him fast.

49 And forthwith he came to Jesus, and said, Hail, master; and kissed him.

50 And Jesus said unto him, Friend, wherefore art thou come? Then came they, and laid hands on Jesus, and took him.

51 And, behold, one of them which were with Jesus stretched out his hand, and drew his sword, and struck a servant of the high priest's, and smote off his ear.

52 Then said Jesus unto him, Put up again thy sword into his place: for all they that take the sword shall perish with the sword.

53 Thinkest thou that I cannot now pray to my Father, and he shall presently give me more than twelve legions of angels?

54 But how then shall the scriptures be fulfilled, that thus it must be?

I N Ó M
N I B V S
requiem que
siui : et in here
ditate dómini
morabor. Túc
precepit et di
xit mihi creator omniū : et qui
creauit me, requieuit in taber
naculo meo. Et dixit mihi.
In iacob inhabita : et in israel
hereditare, et in electis meis
mitte radices. Et sic in sion
firmata sum : et in ciuitate
sanctificata similiter requieui;
et in hierusalem potestas mea.

CORINTHIANS

CHAPTER 13

V.1-13

T HOUGH I speak with the tongues of men and of angels, and have not charity, I am become *as* sounding brass, or a tinkling cymbal.

2 And though I have *the gift of* prophecy, and understand all mysteries, and all knowledge; and though I have all faith, so that I could remove mountains, and have not charity, I am nothing.

3 And though I bestow all my goods to feed *the poor,* and though I give my body to be burned, and have not charity, it profiteth me nothing.

4 Charity suffereth long, *and* is kind; charity envieth not; charity vaunteth not itself, is not puffed up.

5 Doth not behave itself unseemly, seeketh not her own, is not easily provoked, thinketh no evil;

6 Rejoiceth not in iniquity but rejoiceth in the truth;

7 Beareth all things, believeth all things, hopeth all things, endureth all things.

8 Charity never faileth: but whether *there be* prophecies, they shall fail; whether *there be* tongues, they shall cease; whether *there be* knowledge, it shall vanish away.

9 For we know in part, and we prophesy in part.

10 But when that which is perfect is come, then that which is in part shall be done away.

11 When I was a child, I spake as a child, I understood as a child, I thought as a child: but when I became a man, I put away childish things.

12 For now we see through a glass, darkly; but then face to face: now I know in part; but then shall I know even as also I am known.

13 And now abideth faith, hope, charity, these three; but the greatest of these *is* charity.

THE

REVELATIONS

OF ST JOHN THE DIVINE

CHAPTER 4

V.1-2, 4-11

AFTER this I looked, and, behold, a door *was* opened in heaven: and the first voice which I heard *was* as it were of a trumpet talking with me; which said, Come up hither, and I will shew thee things which must be hereafter.

2 And immediately I was in the spirit: and, behold, a throne was set in heaven, and *one* sat on the throne.

4 And round about the throne *were* four and twenty seats: and upon the seats I saw four and twenty elders sitting, clothed in white raiment; and they had on their heads crowns of gold.

5 And out of the throne proceeded lightnings and thunderings and voices: and *there were* seven lamps of fire burning before the throne, which are the seven Spirits of God.

6 And before the throne *there was* a sea of glass like unto crystal: and in the midst of the throne, and round about the throne, *were* four beasts full of eyes before and behind.

7 And the first beast *was* like a lion, and the second beast like a calf, and the third beast had a face as a man, and the fourth beast *was* like a flying eagle.

8 And the four beasts had each of them six wings about *him*; and *they were* full of eyes within: and they rest not day and night, saying, Holy, holy, holy, Lord God Almighty, which was, and is, and is to come.

9 And when those beasts give glory and honour and thanks to him that sat on the throne, who liveth for ever and ever.

10 The four and twenty elders fall down before him that sat on the throne, and worship him that liveth for ever and ever, and cast their crowns before the throne, saying,

11 Thou art worthy, O Lord, to receive glory and honour and power: for thou hast created all things, and for thy pleasure they are and were created.

PICTURE CREDITS